# Co[ntents]

D0185229

1

# 1 What are we?

All the creatures on planet Place Value are numbered differently.
Can you work out the numbers on these creatures?

**1**

I am a 2-digit number
whose digits are different.
If you add my digits the answer is 9.
The difference between my digits is 3.
My units digit is
half my tens digit.

**2**

I am a 3-digit number
whose digits are all different.
My units digit is an odd number less than 6.
My tens digit is 6 more than my units digit.
Add my units and tens digits to
get my hundreds digit.

**3**

I am a 3-digit number
whose digits are all different.
My tens digit is double my units digit.
My units digit is odd.
The sum of my digits is 14.

**4**

I am a 4-digit number whose digits are all different. My units digit is double my thousands digit and 1 less than my tens digit. My thousands digit is an odd number. My hundreds digit is the difference between my tens digit and my thousands digit.

**5**

I am a 4-digit number whose digits are all different. My units digit is one third of my thousands digit and 3 less than my hundreds digit. My tens digit is 1 added to half my hundreds digit.

**6**

I am a 5-digit number whose digits are all different. My units digit is double my ten thousands digit and 1 less than my tens digit. My thousands digit is the difference between my tens digit and my ten thousands digit. My hundreds digit is the sum of my ten thousands digit and my units digit. My ten thousands digit is even.

What if my ten thousands digit is odd?

# 2 Sum puzzle

Copy this diagram.

Write each number in a circle. All lines of 3 must have the given total.

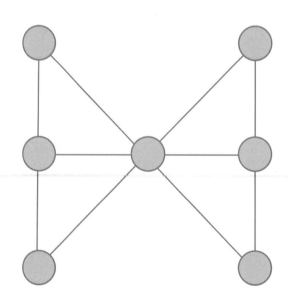

| | | | | | | | | | | |
|---|---|---|---|---|---|---|---|---|---|---|
| **①** | **Numbers:** | 2 | 3 | 4 | 5 | 6 | 7 | 8 | **Line totals:** | 15 |
| **②** | **Numbers:** | 7 | 8 | 9 | 10 | 11 | 12 | 13 | **Line totals:** | 30 |
| **③** | **Numbers:** | 20 | 21 | 22 | 23 | 24 | 25 | 26 | **Line totals:** | 69 |

# 4 Money bags

1. Jenny divided 15 pennies among 4 money bags.

   She could then pay any amount from 1p to 15p just by giving bags.

   How many pennies did Jenny put in each bag?

2. Marcus divided 31 pennies among 5 money bags.

   He could then pay any amount from 1p to 31p just by giving bags.

   a   How many pennies did Marcus put in each bag?

   b   Can you see a relationship between the amounts of money in the bags?
   Describe the relationship.

   c   What if Marcus has one more money bag?
   What is the smallest amount he needs to put in it to make any amount from 1p to 63p?

# 5 Computer crash!

Five children were all playing a game on the computer when the computer crashed and all their scores were lost!

The children remembered the sum of all the scores and of some pairs of scores. They were then able to work out each score.

Can you work out each child's score?

**1** The sum of all the scores was 21.

Ann's score plus Ben's score was 6.

Ben's score plus Ceri's score was 10.

Ceri's score plus Dave's score was 7.

Dave's score plus Elvis's score was 9.

**2** The sum of all the scores was 39.

Ann's score plus Ben's score was 10.

Ben's score plus Ceri's score was 12.

Ceri's score plus Dave's score was 21.

Dave's score plus Elvis's score was 20.

**3** The sum of all the scores was 98.

Ann's score plus Ben's score was 34.

Ben's score plus Ceri's score was 40.

Ceri's score plus Dave's score was 39.

Dave's score plus Elvis's score was 43.

What would the scores be if the total score was:

- 97?

- 99?

# 6 Sponsored walk

Holly, Janine and Vikram have been on a sponsored walk around the school field.

**1** Holly completed 20 laps and raised £5 from 6 sponsors.

Sponsor A paid twice as much as sponsor F.

Sponsor B paid 5p a lap.

Sponsor C paid half of what sponsors A and B paid altogether.

Sponsor D paid the same amount as sponsor E.

Sponsor F paid 4p a lap.

| St Patrick's Primary School Sponsored Walk | |
|---|---|
| Sponsor | Amount |
| | |
| | |
| | |
| | |
| | |
| | |
| | |

a How much did sponsor B pay?

b How much did sponsor F pay?

c How much did sponsors B and F pay altogether?

d How much did sponsor A pay?

e How much did sponsor C pay?

f How much did sponsors A, B, C and F pay altogether?

g How much must sponsors D and E have paid to bring the total to £5?

h How much did sponsors D and E pay each?

**2** Janine completed 34 laps and raised £11.63 from 6 sponsors.

Sponsor A paid twice as much as sponsor F.

Sponsor B paid 5p a lap.

Sponsor C paid half of what sponsors A and B paid altogether.

Sponsor D paid the same amount as sponsor E.

Sponsor F paid 4p a lap.

How much did sponsor E pay?

**3** Vikram completed 69 laps and raised £31.38 from 6 sponsors.

Sponsor A paid twice as much as sponsor F.

Sponsor B paid 8p a lap.

Sponsor C paid half of what sponsors A and B paid altogether.

Sponsor D paid the same amount as sponsor E.

Sponsor F paid 6p a lap.

How much did sponsor E pay?

# 7 Shape mobiles

The children are making shape mobiles from straws.

Each child is making two different shapes.

How many of each shape can each child make from their straws so that there are no straws left over?

Work out all the possibilities.

**1** Ahmed has 34 straws.

He is making triangles and squares.

**2** Jenny has 52 straws.

She is making pentagons and hexagons.

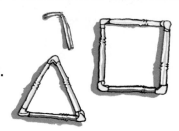

**3** Jack has 70 straws.

He is making hexagons and octagons.

# 8 Number line race

Fred Frog, Freda Frog and Francis Frog are playing a game on a number line.

1. Fred starts at 8. He jumps in 3s.

   Freda starts at –30. She jumps in 4s.

   Francis starts at –46. He jumps in 6s.

   All the frogs jump at the same time.

   Which frog reaches 50 first?

   How many jumps behind are the other frogs?

2. Fred starts at 4. He jumps in 6s.

   Freda starts at –26. She jumps in 9s.

   Francis starts at –98. He jumps in 11s.

   All the frogs jump at the same time.

   Which frog reaches 100 first?

   How many jumps behind are the other frogs?

Can you think of a way of solving the problem without actually having to count?

**Extra challenge**

Which number do Fred and Freda land on at the same time?

# 9 Fair shares

Ben has $\frac{1}{2}$ the number of sweets that Amy has.

Amy doesn't think that is very fair.

She gives 2 of her sweets to Ben.

Now they each have the same number of sweets.

How many sweets did they each start with?

Try different numbers of sweets for Amy.
Each time, work out how many sweets
Ben would have.
How many would they each have if Amy gave
2 sweets to Ben?

# 10  Puzzling symbols

Each symbol represents a number.

Row totals are shown on the right.

Column totals are shown at the bottom.

Work out the missing totals.

**1**

| ◆ | ⊙ | ✸ | ⊙ | ? |
|---|---|---|---|---|
| ✸ | ◆ | ✸ | ◆ | 14 |
| ◆ | ⊙ | ✸ | ◆ | ? |
| ⊙ | ✸ | ✸ | ⊙ | ? |
| ? | 13 | 8 | ? | |

**2**

| ◆ | ⊙ | ✸ | ⊙ | ? |
|---|---|---|---|---|
| ✸ | ◆ | ✸ | ◆ | 30 |
| ◆ | ⊙ | ✸ | ◆ | ? |
| ⊙ | ✸ | ✸ | ⊙ | ? |
| ? | 29 | 24 | ? | |

**3**

| ◆ | ⊙ | ✸ | ⊙ | ? |
|---|---|---|---|---|
| ✸ | ◆ | ✸ | ◆ | 78 |
| ◆ | ⊙ | ✸ | ◆ | ? |
| ⊙ | ✸ | ✸ | ⊙ | ? |
| ? | 77 | 72 | ? | |

**Extra challenge**

Add all the row totals.

Predict the sum of all the column totals.

Is your prediction right?

# 11 Seating arrangements

Some children are arranging square tables for a party.

They can be used to seat 4 children – one at each side like this:

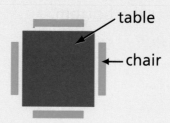

table

chair

Or the tables can be joined to make lines:

seats 6

seats 8 . . . and so on

Find ways to seat the numbers of children given below without having any empty places.

**1** 14 children using 4 tables

**2** 16 children using 5 tables

**3** 32 children using 10 tables

**4** 44 children using 15 tables

# 12 Secret code

In a sequence of coloured flags, each flag represents a letter.

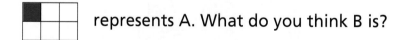 represents A. What do you think B is?

Can you work out what this coded message says?

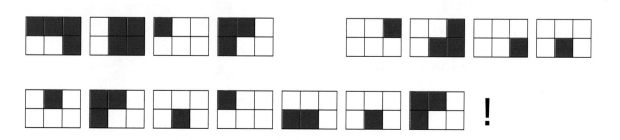

# 13 Palindromic investigation

A **palindrome** is a word or number that reads the same forwards and backwards. These are **palindromic numbers**:

| 77 | 99 | 131 | 464 | 7227 | 9009 | 37 573 |
|----|----|-----|-----|------|------|--------|

Choose a number: 29

Reverse the digits: 92

Add the two numbers.

The answer is a **palindrome.**

We reached a palindrome in one stage (one addition).

```
   29
+  92
  121
```

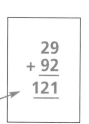

Choose a number: 84

Reverse the digits: 48

Add the two numbers.

The answer is **not** a **palindrome.**

Reverse the digits of the total.

Add the two numbers.

The answer **is** a **palindrome.**

We reached a palindrome in two stages (two additions).

```
    84
+   48
   132
+  231
   363
```

**1** Which of these numbers produces a palindrome:

- in 1 stage?

- in 2 stages?

| | | | | |
|---|---|---|---|---|
| **18** | **26** | **38** | 45 | 53 |
| 64 | 65 | **76** | **85** | **94** |

**2** Can you find any more 1-stage and 2-stage numbers?

**3** Investigate numbers to 100.

Which numbers are already palindromes?

Which numbers take 1, 2, 3 . . . stages to produce a palindrome?

Are there any numbers that do not produce a palindrome?

Which numbers take the most stages?

Record your investigation carefully.

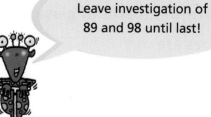

Leave investigation of 89 and 98 until last!

# 14 Windows

Pradesh makes stained glass windows.

He has some square wooden frames and squares of red and white glass.

How many different windows can he make if in each window:

**1**

- there are 9 squares of glass
- 6 squares are red
- no 3 red squares are in line.

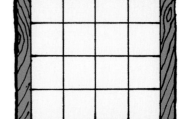

**2**

- there are 16 squares of glass
- 8 squares are red
- no 3 red squares are in line.

# 15 Number neighbours

Numbers that are next to each other when we count are called consecutive numbers.

## 4, 5, 6, 7 are consecutive numbers.

## 57, 58, 59, 60, 61 are consecutive numbers.

We can make some numbers by adding consecutive numbers:

$19 = 9 + 10$       $12 = 3 + 4 + 5$       $36 = 11 + 12 + 13$

**1** Investigate totals up to 20 that can be made by adding:

a   2 consecutive numbers.

b   3 consecutive numbers.

**2** Investigate totals up to 30 that can be made by adding consecutive numbers.

Can you find any numbers that are the sum of more than 3 consecutive numbers?

**3** Investigate totals up to 40 that can be made by adding consecutive numbers.

Some things to think about:
- the best way of recording
- patterns
- how you add numbers
- numbers that can't be shown as the sum of consecutive numbers.

# 16 PE purchases

Mr Fitman the PE teacher bought balls, PE mats and hoops.

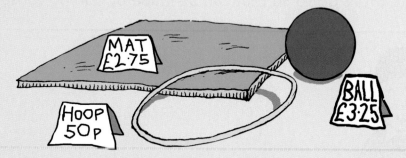

MAT £2·75

HOOP 50p

BALL £3·25

He bought the same number of balls and hoops.

How many of each item did he buy if he spent:

**1** £27 altogether?

**2** £40 altogether?

# 17 Area challenge

These polygons each have an area of 4 square centimetres.

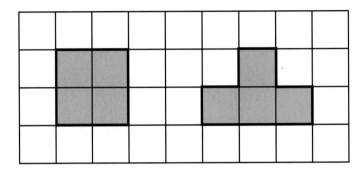

You need centimetre squared or dotty paper.

1. How many different polygons with an area of 4 square centimetres can you find?

2. How many symmetrical polygons with an area of 4 square centimetres can you find? Draw the lines of symmetry.

3. How many other shapes with an area of 4 square centimetres can you find?

Record all your polygons carefully.

Underneath each shape write its name if you can.

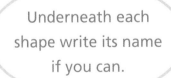

You could have a competition with some friends to see who can find the most shapes.

# 18 Dog run

Jack has some trees in his garden.

He wants to join 3 of the trees with fences to make a triangular area for his dog to play in.

How many different triangles are possible if Jack has:

**①** 4 trees?

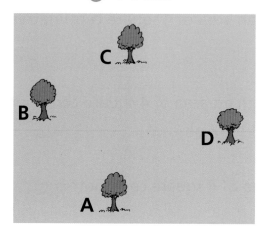

**②** 5 trees?

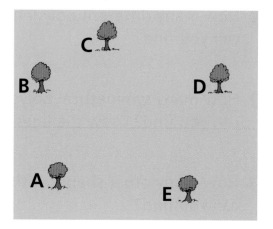

**③** 6 trees?

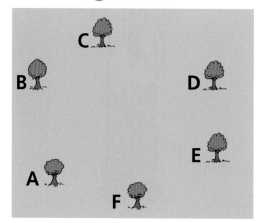

④ Freya has 7 trees in her garden.

She wants to join 4 of the trees with fences to make a quadrilateral area for her dog to play in.

How many different quadrilaterals are possible?

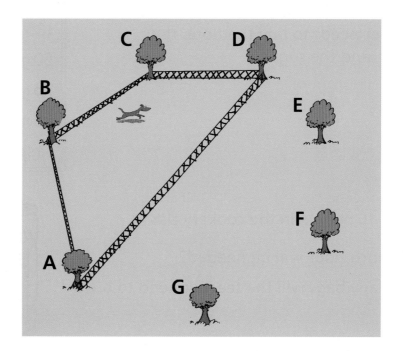

# 19 Ginger biscuits

Each person in a cookery class is going to make 10 ginger biscuits.

The teacher needs to buy the flour, the margarine and the sugar.

Ingredients for 10 ginger biscuits

125 g flour

50 g margarine

75 g sugar

25 ml syrup

1 tsp ground ginger

**1** There are 10 people in the cookery class.

a How much flour will be needed?

b How many bags will the teacher need to buy?

c How much margarine will be needed?

d How many tubs will the teacher need to buy?

e How much sugar will be needed?

f How many bags will the teacher need to buy?

g How much will the teacher pay altogether for the flour, margarine and sugar he buys?

h How much change will he get from £10?

Use the recipe on page 24 to find out how much change the teacher will get from £10 if:

**2** there are 20 people in the cookery class.

**3** there are 25 people in the cookery class.

Flour is sold in 1.5 kg bags.

A bag of sugar costs 69p.

Sugar is sold in 1 kg bags.

A 250 g tub of margarine costs 75p.

A bag of flour costs 72p.

# 20 Wristbands

Jack has a bag of beads to make wristbands.

**1** With the beads he could make wristbands with:

2 beads on each but have 1 bead left over

3 beads on each and have no beads left over

5 beads on each and have no beads left over

4 beads on each but have 1 bead left over

There are fewer than 50 beads in the bag.
How many beads are there?

**2** With the beads he could make wristbands with:

2 beads on each and have no beads left over

3 beads on each and have no beads left over

5 beads on each but have 2 beads left over

7 beads on each but have 2 beads left over

There are fewer than 100 beads in the bag.
How many beads are there?

# 21 Grid totals

**1** Copy this grid.

The numbers at the side are the row totals.

The numbers underneath are the column totals.

Write numbers in the grid to make row and column totals correct.

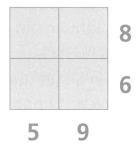

Here is one solution:

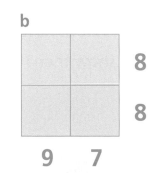

How many other solutions can you find?

**2** Investigate solutions to these:

a

b

c

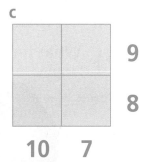

**3** Make up some grids of your own to investigate.

Think and write about:
• why some grids have more solutions than others
• how to predict how many solutions a grid will have
• how to make up your own grid.

# 22 Quick time

Adam, Natasha and Greg each bought an old analogue clock from the market.

They all set their clocks to the correct time at 12 noon on 1st March.

Unfortunately the clocks are not very accurate!

**1** Adam's clock gains half an hour each day!

What time will it show at 12 noon on:

a  2nd March?          b  4th March?          c  7th March?

d  8th March?

At noon of what date will Adam's clock have gained:

e  4 hours?            f  6 hours?            g  8 hours?

h  On what date will Adam's clock have gained 12 hours?

i  What time will his clock show then?

AND NOW FOR THE MIDDAY NEWS

**2** Natasha's clock gains 15 minutes each day!

On what date will her clock next show 12 o'clock again?

**3** Greg's clock gains 10 minutes each day!

On what date will his clock next show the correct time?

# 23 Winning totals

On these dartboards there are just two numbers.

Use as many darts as you like to get the winning total exactly.

How many different ways can you find?

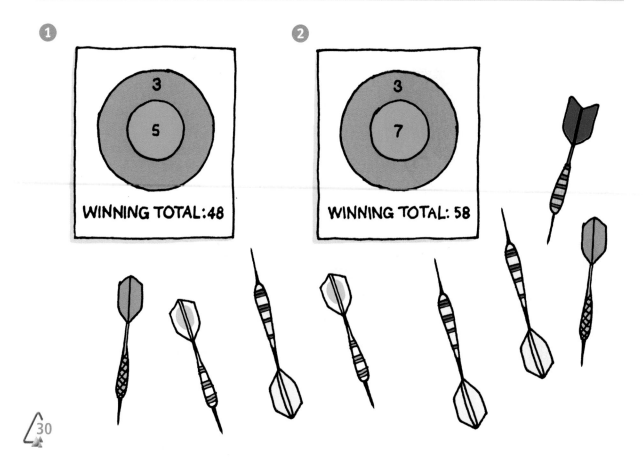

**1**

3
5

**WINNING TOTAL: 48**

**2**

3
7

**WINNING TOTAL: 58**

# 24 Colourful cars

You need PCM 13.

Jamie carried out a survey of the colours of cars passing his school.

He made the bar chart on PCM 13 to show the number of cars for each colour.

He forgot to write the numbers up the vertical axis and the colour for each bar!

Can you do that for him, using what he found out?

**1** There were:

- more white cars than any other colour
- 15 white cars
- 10 grey cars
- 4 more grey cars than blue cars
- 4 more blue cars than yellow cars
- 5 fewer blue cars than red cars
- twice as many black cars as blue cars
- some green cars.

**2** There were:

- 15 more red cars than green cars
- 75 white cars
- 4 times as many green cars as yellow cars
- 3 times as many blue cars as yellow cars
- fewer grey cars than black cars
- more white cars than any other colour.

# 25 Test ramp

Six children made model cars.

They tested them on a ramp to see how far each one would travel.

Use the clues on page 33 to work out which result belongs to which child.

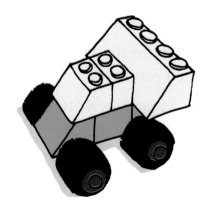

## Results

| 1 | 20 cm | 65 cm | 45 cm | 40 cm | 90 cm | 30 cm |
|---|-------|-------|-------|-------|-------|-------|
| 2 | 65 cm | 1 m 80 cm | 60 cm | 1 m 30 cm | 1 m 55 cm | 2 m 20 cm |
| 3 | 0.53 m | 1.56 m | 0.52 m | 1.06 m | 0.73 m | 1.26 m |

Results

Emily:_____
Hannah:_____
Jake:_____
Meena:_____
Josh:_____
David:_____

# Clues

Jake's car travelled the same distance as the total for Josh and Hannah's cars.

Meena's car travelled one third the distance that David's car travelled.

David's car travelled $\frac{1}{2}$ a metre more than Emily's car.

Hannah's car travelled half the distance that Emily's car travelled.

# 26 The Pizza Place

The Pizza Place has just three tables. Each table is a different size.

The biggest table seats three times as many people as the smallest table.

The middle table seats twice as many people as the smallest table.

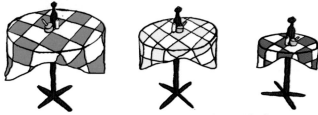

**1** How many people can be seated altogether if the **smallest** table can seat:

a  2 people?       b  3 people?

How many people can be seated altogether if the **middle** table can seat:

c  2 people?       d  8 people?

How many people can be seated altogether if the **biggest** table can seat:

e  15 people?      f  18 people?

g  If the restaurant can seat 24 people altogether, how many seats does each table have?

**2** On Saturday night $\frac{1}{4}$ of the seats were not taken.

12 more people arrived, but there were only enough seats for $\frac{1}{2}$ of them.

How many people altogether does the smallest table seat?

**3** On Saturday night $\frac{3}{4}$ of the seats were taken.

18 more people arrived, but there were only enough seats for $\frac{1}{3}$ of them.

How many people altogether does the smallest table seat?

# 27 Tangrams

You need the tangram pieces cut from PCM 14.

A tangram is a traditional Chinese puzzle.

A square is cut into 7 pieces called 'tans'.

These can be used to make pictures and shapes.

Try making these pictures.

Make the polygons below.

Record how the pieces fitted together so you won't forget.

1 Use B, C and F to make:

  a  a triangle        b  a rectangle.

  Use A, C and F to make:

  c  a square          d  a rectangle.

**2** **a** Use A, B, F and E to make a triangle.

**b** Use A, C, F and G to make a square.

Use C, B, D and F to make:

**c** a rectangle **d** a pentagon.

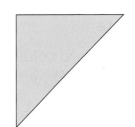

**3** Use A, B, C, D and F to make:

**a** a triangle **b** a square.

Use C, B, E, F and G to make:

**c** a rectangle **d** a hexagon.

**4** Use all of the pieces to make:

**a** a triangle **b** a rectangle.

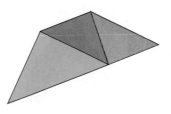

# 28 Last digit patterns

You can make patterns using the last digits of the answers in a times-table.

Here is how to make the × 4 last digit pattern.

Write two columns of digits 0 to 9 on squared paper.

Starting with 1, multiply each number in the left-hand column by 4.

Each time join the number to the last digit of the answer in the right-hand column:

| 1 × 4 = 4 | so join 1 to 4 |
| 2 × 4 = 8 | so join 2 to 8 |
| 3 × 4 = 12 | so join 3 to 2 |
| 4 × 4 = 16 | so join 4 to 6 |

and so on to 9 × 4.

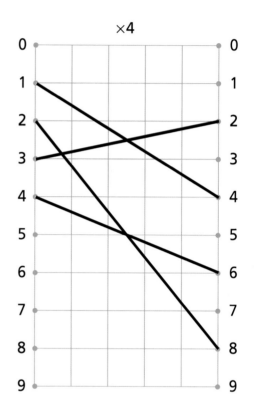

**1** a Copy and complete the × 4 pattern.

   b Draw the patterns for the 2, 3 and 5 times tables.

**2** Investigate patterns for all the times-tables from × 2 to × 9.

Record anything interesting you notice about your patterns.

# 29 Ruritanian Lotto

In Ruritania they have an unusual national lottery.

Winning numbers are decided by the sum of the digits.

Numbers with a zero don't count.

Each week they have a different winning digit sum.

If the winning sum is 4, this number is a winner!

Find all the possible winning numbers if the winning digit sum is:

**1**    a   2        b   3        c   4

**2**   5

**3**   6

# 30 Cutting the cake

Jake is 9 years old today.

His birthday cake has the numbers 0 to 9 equally spaced around the edge.

① Jake cuts one slice out of the cake.

What are the numbers on the slice if they add up to:

a  10?       b  11?       c  13?

d  17?       e  18?       f  21?

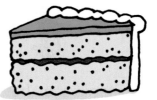

Find as many solutions as you can.

**2** Jake cuts 2 slices out of the cake.

The sums of the numbers on each slice are equal.

What are the numbers on each slice?

Find as many solutions as you can.

**3** Jake makes 3 cuts to cut the whole cake into 3 slices.

The numbers on each slice have the same total.

a   What are the numbers on each slice?

b   What fraction of the whole cake is each slice?

# Glossary

### analogue clock

An analogue clock or watch uses hands to show the time.

### area

The area of a 2-D shape is the amount of space inside it.

Area is usually measured in square units, e.g. *square centimetres* ($cm^2$), square metres ($m^2$).

### axis

the *horizontal* or *vertical* reference line on a *graph*

The plural of axis is axes.

### bar chart

a *graph* in which numbers or measures are represented by the heights of bars

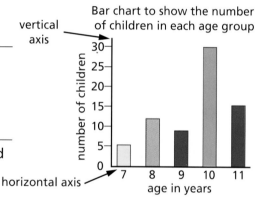

Bar chart to show the number of children in each age group

vertical axis

horizontal axis

### column

a *vertical* (up and down) line of rectangles in a table or rectangular grid

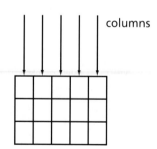

columns

### data

information

## day

a unit of time

A day begins and ends at midnight.

1 day = 24 *hours*

7 days = 1 week

## difference between

The difference between two numbers is how much bigger or smaller one number is than the other.

It can be found by subtracting the smaller number from the larger number, or by counting on from the smaller number to the larger number.

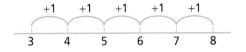

The difference between 3 and 8 is 5.

## digit

The digits are **0 1 2 3 4 5 6 7 8 9**.

All numbers have one or more digits.

The digits of 52 are 5 and 2.

The position of a digit in a number tells us its value.

## double

twice as many; to multiply by 2

Double 6 is 6 × 2 = 12.

## even number

a number that can be divided exactly by 2

Even numbers end in 0, 2, 4, 6 or 8.

78 and 654 are even numbers.

## fewer

not as many as, or a smaller number of

A bird has fewer legs than a dog.

## fraction

a part of a whole shape or number

A *half* ($\frac{1}{2}$) and a *quarter* ($\frac{1}{4}$) are fractions.

## graph

a type of diagram showing the relationship between *data*

> Block graphs and *bar charts* are types of graph.

## half ($\frac{1}{2}$)

a *fraction*

> When you divide a shape or number into 2 equal parts, each part is a half ($\frac{1}{2}$).

A half ($\frac{1}{2}$)
of this circle is red.

half ($\frac{1}{2}$)    half ($\frac{1}{2}$)

A half ($\frac{1}{2}$) of 6 is 3.

## hexagon

a *polygon* with 6 sides

hexagons

## horizontal

from side to side without slanting

a horizontal line

## hour

a unit of time

> 1 hour = 60 *minutes*
>
> 24 hours = 1 *day*

## hundreds digit

the third digit from the right in a whole number

hundreds digit

6497

## investigate

to find out all you can about something

## kilogram

a unit of mass

> 1 kilogram = 1000 grams

## line symmetry, line of symmetry

When you can draw a line across a shape or pattern so that each side of the shape or pattern is a reflection of the other side, we say it has line symmetry. The line is called the line of symmetry or mirror line.

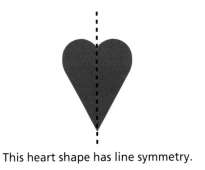

This heart shape has line symmetry.

## metre

a unit of length

> 1 metre = 100 centimetres or
> 1000 millimetres

## minute

a unit of time

> 1 minute = 60 seconds
>
> 60 minutes = 1 *hour*

## noon

12 o'clock in the middle of the *day*

## octagon

a *polygon* with 8 sides

## odd number

a number that cannot be divided exactly by 2

> Odd numbers end in 1, 3, 5, 7 or 9.
>
> 69 and 473 are odd numbers.

octagons

## pentagon

a *polygon* with 5 sides

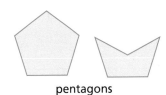

pentagons

## polygon

a 2-D shape with straight sides

> These are all polygons.

polygons

## possibility

whatever is possible

> If the *sum* of a pair of numbers is 4, then it is possible that the numbers are 0 and 4, 1 and 3 or 2 and 2. So 0 and 4, 1 and 3, 2 and 2 are all possibilities. 1 and 5 is **not** a possibility because the sum of 1 and 5 is not 4.

## predict

to use information to work out what you think will happen

## quarter ($\frac{1}{4}$)

a *fraction*

> When you divide a shape or number into 4 equal parts, each part is a quarter ($\frac{1}{4}$).

| quarter ($\frac{1}{4}$) | quarter ($\frac{1}{4}$) |
|---|---|
| quarter ($\frac{1}{4}$) | quarter ($\frac{1}{4}$) |

A quarter ($\frac{1}{4}$) of this rectangle is yellow.

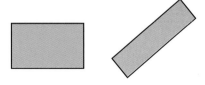

A quarter ($\frac{1}{4}$) of 8 is 2.

## rectangle

a *polygon* in which all 4 angles are right angles and opposite sides are equal

## relationship

a way in which things are connected

> One relationship between 1, 13, 15 and 23 is that they are all *odd numbers*.

## row

a *horizontal* (side to side) line of rectangles in a table or rectangular grid

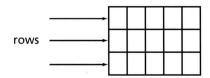

rows

## solution

the answer to a problem

## square

a *rectangle* in which all 4 sides are equal

## square centimetre

a *square* with sides of one centimetre

A square centimetre (cm²) is a unit of *area*.

1 cm

1 cm

## sum

the result of adding numbers

The sum of 7 and 3 is 10. (See also *total*.)

## survey

When you collect *data* you are carrying out a survey.

## symbol

a sign or letter that stands for something

> is a symbol that means 'greater than'.

## tens digit

the second digit from the right in a whole number

ten thousands digit          tens digit

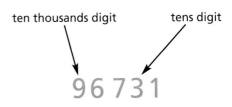

96 731

## ten thousands digit

the fifth digit from the right in a whole number

## third ($\frac{1}{3}$)

a *fraction*

When you divide a shape or number into 3 equal parts, each part is a third ($\frac{1}{3}$).

A third ($\frac{1}{3}$) of this circle is red.

A third ($\frac{1}{3}$) of 9 is 3.

## thousands digit

the fourth digit from the right in a whole number

thousands digit

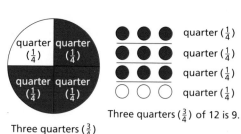

7615

## three quarters ($\frac{3}{4}$)

When a shape or number has been divided into 4 equal parts each part is a *quarter* ($\frac{1}{4}$). Three of the parts are three quarters ($\frac{3}{4}$).

quarter ($\frac{1}{4}$)
quarter ($\frac{1}{4}$)
quarter ($\frac{1}{4}$)
quarter ($\frac{1}{4}$)

Three quarters ($\frac{3}{4}$) of 12 is 9.

Three quarters ($\frac{3}{4}$) of this circle is red.

## total

the result of adding numbers

The total of 4 and 5 is 9. (See also *sum*.)

## triangle

a *polygon* with 3 sides

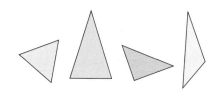

## two thirds ($\frac{2}{3}$)

When a shape or number has been divided into 3 equal parts each part is a *third* ($\frac{1}{3}$). Two of the parts are two thirds ($\frac{2}{3}$).

third ($\frac{1}{3}$)
third ($\frac{1}{3}$)
third ($\frac{1}{3}$)

Two thirds ($\frac{2}{3}$) of this rectangle is blue.

Two thirds ($\frac{2}{3}$) of 6 is 4.

## units digit

the digit at the right-hand end of a whole number

units digit

3209

## vertical

straight up and down without slanting

a vertical line